T0208722

Speaking Life Over Our Children One Letter at a Time

Lisa Moises

WESTBOW°
PRESS
A DIVISION OF THOMAS NELSON
& ZONDERVAN

WestBow Press books may be ordered through booksellers or by contacting:

WestBow Press
A Division of Thomas Nelson & Zondervan
1663 Liberty Drive
Bloomington, IN 47403
www.westbowpress.com
1 (866) 928-1240

ISBN: 978-1-4908-5094-8 (sc)
ISBN: 978-1-4908-5093-1 (e)

Library of Congress Control Number: 2014915904

Printed in the United States of America.

WestBow Press rev. date: 10/15/2014

Contents

Introduction vii

A Abound 1

B Blood 3

B The Blessing 5

C Compassion 7

D Doer 9

E Eternal 11

F Faith 13

F Forgive 15

G Grace 17

H Healed 19

I I Am 21

J Joy 23

K Kingdom 25

L Love 27

M Mercy 29

N New 31

O Obey 33

P Praise 35

Q Quicken 37

R Resurrection Power 39

S Saved 41

T   Tithe 43

U   Understanding 45

V   Victory 47

W   Wisdom 49

W   Word of God..51

X   (E)xceedingly 53

Y   Yes...55

Z   Zealous 57

Conclusion...59

Introduction

In our home, we have a poster hanging on one of our bedroom doors that speaks of the promises of God over our children. Every day as I pass by, I declare these words over our three boys. "Lo, children are an heritage of the LORD: and the fruit of the womb is his reward. As arrows are in the hand of a mighty man; so are children of the youth. Happy is the man that hath his quiver full of them: they shall not be ashamed, but they shall speak with the enemies in the gate" (Psalm 127:3–5 KJV).

One day, as I was declaring these particular verses, the Lord stopped me. He spoke to my spirit and revealed something so important that I hadn't realized before. He showed me that the reason there's such an attack on our children today is because once you get children so full of the Word of God, their faith becomes strong, and they become so powerful in the authority of Jesus. When they know who they are in Christ, they're determined to take their rightful authority over Satan and every part of the curse.

And this Word is not limited to our biological children, but is meant for every child the Lord has moved on our hearts to pray for, teach, speak life into, and declare as God's own heritage. This Word is for each child who knows and loves Jesus, and for those whom we believe will come to know Jesus. This Word is for every child represented in the kingdom of God.

It's time for us to take a stand for our children and hold them up in faith. We must speak life over them. We must daily declare the Word of God over our children. Jesus spoke only what the Father told Him to speak. Our words, too, must be the same.

God's Word + Our Words = Children—A Heritage of the Lord!

Author's Note: There are three letters represented twice herein: B for Blood and The Blessing, F for Faith and Forgive, and W for Wisdom and the Word of God. This is because both topics are essential, and you can't have one without the other.

Abound

"And God is able to make all grace abound toward you, that you, always having all sufficiency in all things, may have an abundance for every good work" (2 Corinthians 9:8 NKJV).

I say, my children, abound in grace!

Abounding Grace

Grace abounds for you and for me,
The hand of God's favor for all to see,
When our needs are met, we abound, it's true,
Reaching out to others to refresh and renew.

The grace of God for our children we speak,
That they may help the poor and comfort the weak.
They distribute the love God has for all,
Abounding in grace by answering His call.

To touch the lives of those in need,
Is the plan of God for our generational seed,
That they may show love and openly share
The Good News of Jesus to folks everywhere!

Blood

"And they overcame him by the blood of the Lamb and by the word of their testimony" (Revelation 12:11 NKJV).

I say, my children are covered under the precious blood of Jesus!

The Power of the Blood

The power of the blood, no man can contain,
Not even Satan can hold back and refrain.
For the blood of Jesus was shed for us all,
To redeem our lives from the curse and the fall.

The crown of thorns that pierced His head,
Jesus—whipped, bloodied, and left for dead,
Died on a cross for the world to see;
Jesus shed His blood for you and for me.

This precious blood protects us today
From Satan's evil and twisted way.
Those who choose to be kept free,
Shall walk in The Blessing—the way it
should be!

The Blessing

"The blessing of the LORD makes one rich, and He adds no sorrow with it" (Proverbs 10:22 NKJV).

I say, my children, walk in The Blessing of Abraham!

The Blessing Continued

Jesus restored all that Adam lost,
As He hung innocently on that blood-stained cross,
To redeem our lives from destruction and sin,
To stir up The Blessing deep from within.

The Blessing is Jesus brought back to life
By the power of God and His sacrifice.
He gave up His Son for the world to see,
To restore The Blessing for all eternity.

Our children are heirs of His promise, too,
To receive The Blessing and life renewed.
And as they are blessed through Jesus' grace,
In return, they bless others of this whole human
race.

Compassion

"But when He saw the multitudes He was moved with compassion for them, because they were weary and scattered, like sheep having no shepherd" (Matthew 9:36 NKJV).

I say, my children, overflow with the compassion of Jesus!

The Cause of Christ

God's deep love welled within,
A man of suffering who knew no sin,
Jesus Christ, God's true Son,
Loved unconditionally everyone.

When people mocked and criticized Him,
To refrain from anger and commit no sin,
Jesus healed with compassion instead,
And continued to do what the Father said.

Our children, too, have compassion, you see,
To complete the work the Father gave thee:
To bring healing and wholeness from the Father's hand,
And to spread the love of Jesus throughout this dying land.

Doer

"But he who looks into the perfect law of liberty and continues in it, and is not a forgetful hearer but a doer of the work, this one will be blessed in what he does" (James 1:25 NKJV).

I say, my children, be doers of the Word of God!

Doing What God Commands

The Spirit, the Father, and Jesus, His Son,
Three Eternal Powers all wrapped into one,
With Jesus being born in the form of a man
To complete the assignment of God's ultimate plan.

To redeem mankind and all that was lost,
By obeying the Father at all cost,
To only do what the Father commands,
And willingly pay for sin's selfish demands.

So we continue in the Father's plan, too,
Declaring our children will act and will do
According to the Word that Jesus proclaimed,
Being doers of His Word unashamed.

Eternal

"And this is eternal life, that they may know You, the only true God, and Jesus Christ whom You have sent" (John 17:3 NKJV).

I say, my children, have eternal life in Jesus!

Jesus Gives Us Eternal Life

Who would have thought that this simple man,
Was God's perfect choice in fulfilling His plan
To save mankind from sin and death,
As He hung on the cross and breathed His last breath?

Jesus Christ, our Savior and King,
Freed us from every wicked, accursed thing.
The Blessing's now ours, eternal life, too,
Through Jesus, our Lord, for me and for you.

Our children, we declare, believe in His name,
And the benefits of God are theirs to proclaim.
They choose life everlasting and new,
And reflect God's love in all that they do.

Faith

"So Jesus answered and said to them, 'Have faith in God. For assuredly, I say to you, whoever says to this mountain, 'Be removed and be cast into the sea,' and does not doubt in his heart, but believes that those things he says will be done, he will have whatever he says'" (Mark 11:22–23 NKJV).

I say, my children, have mountain-moving faith!

The Force of Faith

Faith in God can move anything,
Any problem or trouble the devil might bring.
It's the force that moves with power and might
To uproot those mountains clear out of sight.

God's hand moves through faith's full force,
And keeps us on a steady course,
To walk in The Blessing, whole and complete,
To walk in The Blessing and not in defeat.

Unrelenting faith is for us to believe,
That every promise of God is ours to receive
And as faith is firm in our children's hearts,
His Word planted deep will *never* depart!

 **Forgive**

"And be kind to one another, tenderhearted, forgiving one another, even as God in Christ forgave you" (Ephesians 4:32 NKJV).

I say, my children, be quick to forgive!

Forgive Like Jesus

Jesus knew the power of love,
For He was sent from God above
To save mankind from the wages of sin,
Declare us free, washed from within.

Jesus' life, in His Father's hands,
Completed His assignment and followed God's commands
To give up His life and make all things new,
To forgive and to love as we ought to do.

Our children love, too, with the compassion of Christ;
They are quick to forgive, though the world may entice
And say that revenge is the way to be free,
But our children know Jesus, His forgiveness is key.

Grace

"And He said to me, 'My grace is sufficient for you'" (2 Corinthians 12:9 NKJV).

I say, God's grace is sufficient for my children!

Great Grace

The depth of God's love, we freely receive
Through the gift of His grace to all who believe.
We're not judged as we should be, for it is by grace
Through the mercy of God, Jesus stands in our place,

So free and so full, God's favor abounds
Through the shed blood of Jesus and the life He laid down.
Because Jesus took our guilt, sin, and shame,
We're now righteous to God, standing firm in His name,

Our children are blessed with this gift of grace,
As they stand in Jesus, their sins erased
And knowing that God forever loves them true,
Through grace, they'll accomplish what God
calls them to do.

Healed

"But he was wounded for our transgressions, He was bruised for our iniquities; the chastisement for our peace was upon Him, and by His stripes we are healed" (Isaiah 53:5 NKJV).

I say, my children are healed and whole!

Jesus, Our Healer

Jesus knew the cost was high
To redeem mankind from the devil's lie.
From sin and darkness, the curse itself,
He willingly took upon Himself.

To bridge the gap between God and man,
Jesus fulfilled God's perfect plan
To restore our lives and make us whole,
To bring back The Blessing that Satan once stole.

By enduring the stripes laid on His back,
Enduring the mocking and brutal attack,
Jesus came to set us free,
Bringing healing and wholeness for our children
to see.

I Am

"And God said to Moses, 'I AM WHO I AM'"
(Exodus 3:14 NKJV)

I say, my children, know the great *I Am*!

The Great *I Am*

God is so good for all to see;
He loves each one of us so tenderly.
His desire is to bless with abundance and grace,
And shelter us always in His secret place.

There is none like Him; He rules over all,
Ever ready to answer His children's call.
Power and might come from His hands,
As He leads and instructs through His
commands.

When we speak of His wondrous love to our seed,
They'll look to Him to meet every need,
And seek His face, giving Him honor that's due,
For He is our God, most holy and true.

Joy

"You will show me the path of life; in Your presence is fullness of joy" (Psalm 16:11 NKJV).

I say, my children are full of the joy of the Lord!

The Force of Joy

The world today is full of pain,
Sorrow, distress, and feelings of shame,
Worry and anger, anxiety, snares—
A hopeless feeling that no one cares.

Jesus cares and gives us His life,
With His love and His joy that break the world's strife.
He makes us complete, not missing a thing.
From the depths of our hearts, we rejoice and we sing,

Our children need Jesus every day of their lives
To overcome challenges, and not just survive,
But to walk in The Blessing, joy-filled to the brim,
So others may know Jesus and cast their cares
upon Him.

 **Kingdom**

"But seek first the kingdom of God and His righteousness, and all these things shall be added to you" (Matthew 6:33 NKJV).

I say, my children, live in the kingdom of God *now*!

The Kingdom of God

The kingdom of God—what can compare?
We seek first His face so that we can all share
In The Blessing and grace that sets us free,
Abounding in love and God's liberty.

Where Jesus is King and His Word is held true,
We follow Him in all that we do.
Committing to Jesus, surrendering our lives,
Every need's met; as believers, we thrive.

The kingdom of God is for our children, too,
And they will flourish in all that they do.
They tell of their freedom, bought with a price,
As they impact the world for our Lord, Jesus
Christ.

 **Love**

"Beloved, let us love one another, for love is of God" (1 John 4:7 NKJV).

I say, my children, love with the love of God!

Unconditional Love

God loved us before we were born,
Created us special, in His image we're formed.
Intricate details of our frame so complete,
From the top of our heads to the soles of our feet.

And though man sinned, and we were set apart,
We never left the Father's heart.
He gave up His Son so that we could be free,
Forever included in His family.

God's tender love, and Jesus', too,
Washes us clean and makes us brand new.
It opens the door for our children to see
Unconditional love; that's how it *must* be.

Mercy

"Let us therefore come boldly to the throne of grace, that we may obtain mercy and find grace to help in time of need" (Hebrews 4:16 NKJV).

I say, my children, receive mercy from God's throne of grace!

The Mercy of God

The world is in such an evil state,
That many believe in a hopeless fate:
Calamity, confusion, and the problems they bring,
Inflict the wounds of Satan's merciless stings.

But God had perfected a glorious plan,
Rich with His love and merciful hand,
To bring life through Jesus for all in despair,
Lavish His love through His tender care.

Our children know Jesus, so full and so free,
As they rise up and serve Him faithfully.
Remember their covenant of mercy and grace;
It was Jesus who willingly pleaded their case.

New

Therefore, if anyone is in Christ, he is a new creation; old things have passed away, behold, all things have become new" (2 Corinthians 5:17 NKJV).

I say, my children are new creations in Christ!

A New Creation in Jesus

What can Jesus do for you?
Jesus Christ can make you new,
Take away the sin and shame,
Wash away the hurt and blame.

Make us clean and white as snow,
Pour His love so we would know
That Jesus Christ can set us free.
Once we were blind, but now we see

That life with Jesus abounds with joy,
And loosens us from Satan's ploy
To seek God's face and put Him first,
To walk in The Blessing and never the curse!

Obey

"If you are willing and obedient, you shall eat the good of the land" (Isaiah 1:19 NKJV).

I say, my children, obey the Word of God!

Obedience Is the Key

God is speaking; we must obey,
Always following what He will say.
For He knows what's best for us,
In His plans, we *fully* trust.

And though our natural minds say no,
Obedience to God is what we show
By doing exactly what He asks us to,
And using our faith to guide us through.

His ways are perfect, His blessings sure;
As we obey Him, our lives are secure.
And not ourselves only—our children as well;
Obedience is the key; in The Blessing we dwell.

Praise

"Every day I will bless You, and will praise Your name forever and ever" (Psalm 145:2 NKJV).

I say, my children, continually give God praise!

Praise and Thanksgiving to God

To God be all our joyful praise,
He gives us children to love and raise.
With thankful hearts we bless His name,
And teach our children to do the same.

We praise our God for all He's done,
Especially in giving us His only Son.
We come together in one accord
To acknowledge forever that Jesus is *Lord!*

With lifted hands and joyful song,
We know to which family we belong.
We're heirs with Jesus, and can't deny
All praise and glory to God Most High!

Quicken

"… quicken me according to thy word" (Psalm 119:154 KJV).

I say, the Word of God quickens my children!

Quicken Me

When life's hard and we're running low,
The Word of God renews our flow
To walk in love and faith grown strong—
Back on track where we belong.

And though the world may make a fuss,
The Word of God will quicken us
To heal, and love, and be set free
To walk in triumphant victory.

Our children know God's Word is true;
It quickens them in all they do.
We're overcomers, they will say,
For they are blessed in every way.

Resurrection Power

"He is not here, but is risen!" (Luke 24:6 NKJV)

I say, my children have resurrection power!

He *Is* Risen!

Jesus Christ rose from the dead,
Came back to life, just as He said.
He gives His Spirit to make us bold,
With power and authority, His truth is told

That Jesus Christ is Lord of all,
And saved us from man's wicked fall,
To raise us up with power and might—
Victorious in this heavenly fight.

With our children we firmly stand,
Taking hold of God's command
To tell the world that Jesus lives.
The love of God He freely gives.

Saved

"'Sirs, what must I do to be saved?' So they said, 'Believe on the Lord Jesus and you will be saved, you and your household'" (Acts 16:30–31 NKJV).

I say, my children are saved!

Saved through Jesus

The world's road is a hard one to take,
With constant reminders of all our mistakes.
Trying our best, though it's never enough,
No one to help us when life becomes rough.

But Jesus is here, always willing and ready,
Holding on tight, keeping us steady,
Loving us through His mercy and grace,
Without condemnation— not even a trace.

Just believe in the Lord, and saved you will be,
For He died on the cross for you and for me,
To be our Lord, and Savior, and friend,
To be with us always—from now to the end.

Tithe

"'Bring all the tithes into the storehouse, that there may be food in My house, and try Me now in this,' says the LORD of hosts, 'If I will not open for you the windows of heaven and pour out for you such blessing that there will not be room enough to receive it'" (Malachi 3:10 NKJV).

I say, my children are tithers and givers!

The Command to Tithe

Give to the Lord your first 10 %;
Do it before your monies are spent,
So that He can open heaven's windows for you,
Enabling The Blessing to flow right through.

And when it's a challenge, don't stop and quit;
That's the time before the Lord we sit
To stir up our faith and stand on His Word,
And hold on tight to what we've heard,

That God is faithful to those who give,
As He commanded us to live.
To honor Him in all we do,
Our children are tithers and givers, too.

Understanding

"The fear of the LORD is the beginning of wisdom; a good understanding have all those who do His commandments" (Psalm 111:10 NKJV).

I say, my children have a good understanding of who God is in their lives!

Knowing God

God is so great; how awesome is He?
Loving His children so tenderly,
Giving us life, we're the joy of His heart,
Keeping us close and never to part.

His plans for His children, so perfect His will,
For those who'll listen and always be still,
Knowing God's voice and the word that He speaks
And follow His ways; only His face we seek.

To put His Word first in every part of our lives,
Makes it take root, watch it grow, watch it thrive,
And bring forth The Blessing, as He promised
He would,
To those who obey and do as they should.

Victory

"But thanks be to God, who gives us the victory through our Lord Jesus Christ" (1 Corinthians 15:57 NKJV).

I say, my children, have victory in Jesus!

We Are Victorious!

Father, we praise You for Your mercy and grace,
Gave us Your Son, and He took our place.
He endured all the sufferings; it should have been us.
Instead, it was Jesus; it's His name we trust.

Jesus won victory through His death on a cross,
The devil defeated, sins' power now lost
Yes, thanks be to God for Jesus, His Son,
Victory over death for everyone!

For me and my house, I truly declare
That Jesus is Lord; His life we now share.
He gives power and authority to those who
believe,
And victorious living for all who receive.

Wisdom

"Wisdom is the principal thing; therefore get wisdom" (Proverbs 4:7 NKJV).

I say, my children are filled with the wisdom of God!

True Wisdom

For those who know God, we're the apple of His eyes,
Holding fast to His Word, for that makes us wise.
Knowing the power that each Word contains,
Renews our minds, so we're never the same.

We inquire of God for His wisdom each day,
And are willing to listen, to follow, and obey.
For His Word is true; His plans are just right.
When we ask for His wisdom, revelation's in sight.

And we will seek God for our children's lives—yes,
As we follow His wisdom, our children are blessed.
And as they are blessed, they will help others know
Jesus, our Savior, whose healing love flows.

Word of God

"And the Word became flesh and dwelt among us" (John 1:14 NKJV).

I say, my children are anchored in the Word of God!

Jesus, the Word

Jesus, the Word, of flesh He became,
Gave us true life through the power of His name.
He is the Word that God declares just.
His promises are sure; in faith we do trust.

Our lives are anchored in the Word of God.
He leads us, guides us with a shepherd's rod,
And holds us close with love and grace,
Keeps us in step with His steady pace.

So never give up, and never give in;
Leaning on the Word gives us peace from within.
It strengthens our hearts to share the Good News.
For the life-giving Word, it's Jesus we choose.

(E)xceedingly

"After these things the word of the LORD came to Abram in a vision, saying, 'Do not be afraid, Abram. I am your shield, your exceedingly great reward'" (Genesis 15:1 NKJV).

I say, my children know God as their exceedingly great reward!

Exceedingly Blessed

Follow God with all our hearts,
And He will give us a brand new start.
Look to Him in all we do,
He's the One to bring us through.

Life in Him is surely blessed,
For with Him, He gives the best
To those who follow and obey.
In His presence we always stay.

Look to God, *exceeding* love;
We're blessed so richly from above
His goodness is so vast, so great,
That no man can *ever* calculate.

Yes

"For all the promises of God in Him are Yes, and in Him Amen, to the glory of God through us" (2 Corinthians 1:20 NKJV).

I say, my children, say yes to the promises of God!

Yes in Jesus

Jesus died for our sins,
And through His death, in life, we win.
Proclaim His name so all can hear
He crushed the darkness and the fear.

To let the light of God's Word shine,
His faithful promises are yours and mine.
To hold on to God with all our might,
Make all the wrongs turn out all right,

And thus our children hold fast the Word,
And speak to those who've never heard
Of God's promises through Jesus Christ,
Who gives us all a brand new life.

Zealous

"Who gave Himself for us, that He might redeem us from every lawless deed and purify for Himself His own special people, zealous for good works" (Titus 2:14 NKJV).

I say, my children are zealous for the good works of God!

Zeal for the Kingdom of God

Our children stand firm in the light of God's grace,
Readying themselves for their heavenly race
To tell the Good News that Jesus is Lord,
Alive with His Word—their spiritual sword.

And able to do mighty works for the King,
With their faith in Jesus, they can do anything!
With joy in their souls and their hearts full of zeal,
The love for their Savior's so true and so real.

A boldness they have that no one can touch,
So full of the Spirit, loving Jesus so much,
Always ready and willing to do what He asks,
Zealous for Jesus in completing their tasks.

Conclusion

God has a glorious plan for our children. They are His heritage, yes—a reward (Psalm 127:3). But how will they know how much He loves them if we don't know His love, too? If you have never made Jesus your Lord and Savior, receive Him now! Just simply say, "Jesus, come into my life. I make you my Lord and Savior. Forgive me of my sins. I repent, Lord, and I give my life to you!" *Then rejoice!* You are now a part of God's magnificent family, a joint-heir with Jesus Christ. And as joint-heirs, we can speak the promises of God over our children (biological or not), knowing that they will come to pass. We have God's guarantee on it.

"No, I will not break my covenant; I will not take back a single word I said" (Psalm 89:34 NLT).

Hallelujah! God is good!

About the Author

Lisa Moises, a mother of three, has worked in the classroom of private schools for twenty four years, teaching children in the early education and elementary levels. She has had the privilege of sharing with students and families about the necessity of holding fast to the promises of God.